# TEXAS

## A PICTORIAL SOUVENIR

CAROL M. HIGHSMITH AND TED LANDPHAIR

# TEXAS

## A PICTORIAL SOUVENIR

# CRESCENT BOOKS

### NEW YORK

THE AUTHORS GRATEFULLY ACKNOWLEDGE
THE SUPPORT PROVIDED BY

HILTON HOTELS CORPORATION

AND

THE ARLINGTON HILTON
THE AUSTIN NORTH HILTON AND TOWERS
THE EL PASO AIRPORT HILTON
THE HILTON PALACIO DEL RIO, SAN ANTONIO
THE UNIVERSITY HILTON, HOUSTON

IN CONNECTION WITH THE COMPLETION OF THIS BOOK

_PAGES 2–3: Big Bend National Park is an awesome but somewhat inaccessible place, far from urban centers. There, the Chisos Mountains jut spectacularly out of the harsh Chihauhuan desert._

This 1999 edition is published by Crescent Books®,
an imprint of Random House Value Publishing, Inc.,
201 East 50th Street, New York, N.Y. 10022.

Crescent Books® and colophon are registered trademarks of
Random House Value Publishing, Inc.

Random House
New York • Toronto • London • Sydney • Auckland
http://www.randomhouse.com/

Printed and bound in China

Library of Congress Cataloging-in-Publication Data
Highsmith, Carol M., 1946–
Texas / Carol M. Highsmith and Ted Landphair.
p. cm. — (A pictorial souvenir)
ISBN 0-517-20494-0
1. Texas—Pictorial works. 2. Texas—Description and travel.
I. Landphair, Ted, 1942– . II. Title. III. Series: Highsmith, Carol M., 1946–
Pictorial souvenir.
F387.H54  1999                                                      98–38558
976.4—dc21                                                          CIP

8  7  6  5  4  3  2  1

Project Editor: Donna Lee Lurker
Designed by Robert L. Wiser, Archetype Press, Inc., Washington, D.C.

# FOREWORD

Texas is big. It's bigger than New York, New Jersey, Pennsylvania, Ohio, Illinois, *and* the six New England states put together. It is also a diverse state with many distinctive topographies as well as different cultures. Yet in the imagination of the world, Texas and its inhabitants conjure up an image of the quintessential and authentic America, one that is almost mythic and bigger than life.

A Texan is readily spotted by an outgoing nature. He or she seems to radiate a *Texan* identity. It is an aura that traces to *Tejas*—an Indian word meaning "friend" or "friendship." The state's citizens don't merely preach old-fashioned values, they live them. Walk down a Texas street and people will say hello. A stranger is "sir" or "ma'am," and an offer of help or a friendly word is sure to be genuine. Self-reliance is in their blood, but standoffishness is not. Texans have been open to different people and new ideas because they have always lived on the edge of the Spanish world, the Anglo world, and on the very brink of the untamed American frontier. Texans are proud of their history, but not mired in it. Living where "seldom is heard a discouraging word," they have always thought positively, welcomed change, and taken risks.

Texas was the only sovereign republic ever to enter the Union when it became a state in 1845, but the most momentous development in its history was the "discovery" of oil in the twentieth century, which altered its course forever. "Black gold" brought fortune, international fame, and larger-than-life characters. Megalopolises soon arose as Texas became the shooting star of the Sunbelt with money, expanding population, and increasing political power.

Swaggering Dallas, one of Texas's youngest cities, is the nation's eighth-largest city. Once a humble trading post, the East Texas Oil Field brought dramatic expansion to Dallas in the 1930s as it served as the financial and technical center for the oil patch. It soon became one of the nation's top-five business and convention cities. Yet it somehow managed to remain the least densely populated major metropolitan area in the world.

The rest of the state offers a startling variety of attractions. Houston has endless points of interest including the Astrodome, the world's first domed stadium. Texarkana's post office, in northeastern Texas, straddles the Texas-Arkansas state line. College Station, on the campus of Texas A&M University, is the home of the George Bush Presidential Library and Museum. In dry West Texas is Big Bend National Park, which covers eleven hundred square miles. In the unabashed cowboy country of the Texas Panhandle, is Amarillo, a city that calls itself the "real Texas." In South Texas, there is the famed King Ranch, which at 825,000 acres is larger than the state of Rhode Island. In El Paso, on the Mexican border, is Ysleta, built in 1681, the state's oldest mission. In San Antonio, there is, of course, the Alamo—always a tourist favorite—and the *Paseo del Rio*—the River Walk—bordered by restaurants, nightclubs, and retail shops.

Texans relish the state's bigness and diversity. It is a state with an endless catalogue of sights, sounds, and memorable people and places. Brash and beautiful, the Lone Star State can be, in the Texas vernacular, a hoot!

*OVERLEAF: Settlers in the Mexican state of Texas turned the old, limestone Alamo mission into a fortress where they made a heroic but fatal stand for independence in 1836.*

"Old (and stuffed) Tex" (above) is the world's largest mounted longhorn, with a horn span of eight feet nine inches. He stands at San Antonio's Buckhorn Museum and Saloon, founded in 1881 by inveterate hunter Albert Friedrich. He built his collection by offering patrons free drinks in exchange for pairs of horns, rattlesnake skins, and stuffed animals of all shapes, sizes, and ferocity. Many of the animals originally featured are now extinct or endangered. Mission San José y San Miguel de Aguayo in San Antonio (right) is regarded as the "Queen of Texas Missions." It was the most prosperous and best fortified of the structures along Mission Trail. Always cooler than the streetscape above, San Antonio's River Walk (overleaf) is especially inviting at breakfast time.

The Port Isabel Lighthouse (above) near Brownsville overlooks Laguna Madre, the narrow strait between the Texas Mainland and South Padre Island. Built in 1835, it operated until 1905. Padre Island is two distinct land masses, separated by the manmade Port Mansfield Channel and unconnected by bridges. South Padre Island is heavily developed with a lively restaurant and nightlife scene. Remote Padre Island—one of the nation's last unspoiled stretches of seashore—makes up 110 miles of the longer northern finger of the island, accessed by causeway from Corpus Christi. Intriguing seashells and glass bottles from across the sea are routinely discovered on the island's Malaquite Beach (right).

The King Ranch sprawls across 825,000 acres of South Texas, an area larger than Rhode Island. On a map, it's a huge, empty white space. Driving through it at night, it's a vast black expanse, the ranch's sixty thousand cattle unseen until morning. Each year, the ranch throws a cowboy breakfast (above), open to the Kingsville community and visitors. Mixing pancake batter are, left to right, Tio Kleberg, Tom B. Saunders, Jay Evans, and Nicho Morales. Volunteers David Pratt and Madelyn Ahrens patrol the event on horseback (opposite), pausing in front of an old building from the days when the King spread was called the Santa Gertrudis Ranch. Civilization is very much in evidence in revitalized Houston (overleaf), which has snapped back from a devastating oil recession with a vengeance. The "real Texas," as Houston calls itself, has become a model of ethnic diversity.

SHUTTLE

APOLLO

LUNAR EVA SUIT

This small suit was worn by Charles "Pete" Conrad
as he walked on the moon during the Apollo 12 mission.

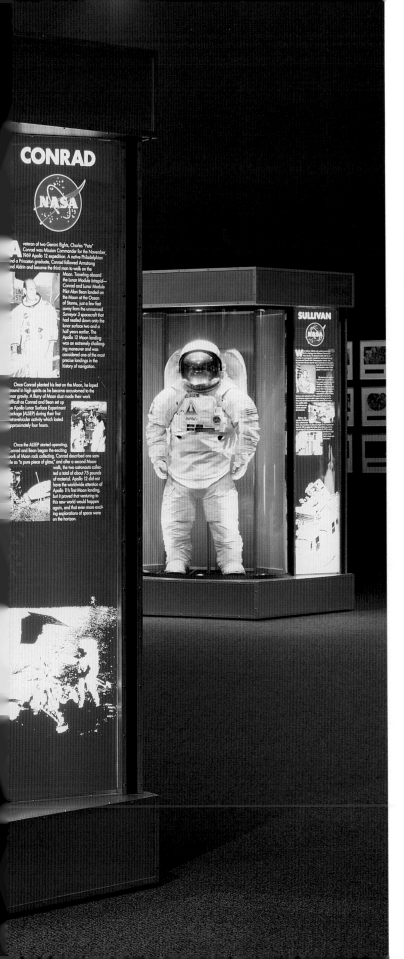

Space Center Houston (left) is a showcase for America's space program. This interactive visitor center for NASA's Johnson Space Center takes guests into the past, present, and future of the nation's astronaut program, with space shuttle mock-ups, IMAX films, and a glimpse of the astronauts in weightlessness training. One of the rites of Texas youth is a pilgrimage to the USS battleship Texas (above), moored in the marshes off Houston's San Jacinto Park. The ship, once the world's most powerful dreadnought, survived a U-boat attack in World War I and supported landings at Normandy and Okinawa in World War II. The Houston Astrodome (overleaf) was the world's first domed stadium when it opened in 1965. It's home to the Houston Astros baseball team, rodeos, and trade shows.

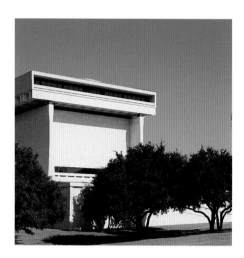

*The Lyndon B. Johnson Library (above) in Austin is the nation's largest and most-visited presidential library. It includes a full-scale replica of the White House Oval Office. Regrettably, the twenty-seven-story University Tower (right), the University of Texas's signature building on its 357-acre Austin campus, has become irrevocably associated with a tragedy: the day in 1966 when deranged honor student Charles Whitman shot forty-four people, killing fourteen, from the Tower's parapet before being shot dead by an off-duty policeman. The dome of the Texas State Capitol (opposite)— the largest state capitol building in the nation—rises seven feet taller than the U.S. Capitol in Washington.*

The Greek Revival Texas Governor's Mansion (above) was constructed of local handmade bricks. Pine logs hauled from Bastrop, Texas, were used to form its six massive pillars. When the mansion opened in 1856, Governor Elisha Pease threw such a "gay and brilliant affair" for three hundred guests that it took him three days to clean up. Pease kept the American Empire sofa, now in the library (opposite), at his private home. Stephen F. Austin's desk occupies another corner. Furnishings have departed, too. Among the possessions that Sam Houston carted home were seventy-five pounds of feathers and eight spittoons. Until Governor John Connally's wife, Idanell, pushed to get an iron fence, brick wall, and security outposts around the mansion, anyone could— and often did— ring the doorbell and roust the governor's family for a chat and an impromptu peek at Houston's old bedroom.

Texans love their Hill Country in the central part of the state, west of Austin. President and Mrs. Lyndon B. Johnson, for instance, returned to their modest home (left) on their working ranch along the Pedernales River at every opportunity. Although Fredericksburg was founded in 1846 by German settlers and retains its German architecture and cuisine in several locations, other European pioneers put their stamp on the community as well. In 1864, Belgian native Felix Van Der Stricken, owner of the town's water-powered gristmill, built his home (above)—now the Market Square Bed & Breakfast Inn—out of native limestone. The bare spot in the distance (overleaf) is the Enchanted Rock State Natural Area, one of Texans' favorite hiking and picnicking areas.

Texas Agricultural and Mechanical, or Texas A&M, University in College Station (above), founded in 1876, is the oldest state university in Texas. It is famed for its military Cadet Corps and ROTC programs, whose graduates served by the thousands in both World Wars, the Korean War, and in Vietnam and Iraq. A&M students good-naturedly bear the bumpkin image as "Aggies," but the nickname belies the school's leadership in agriculture, engineer- ing, and nuclear tech- nology. The George Bush Presidential Library and Museum (left) opened on the Texas A&M Univer- sity campus in College Station in 1997. Its exhibits range from a 1925 home movie of Bush's first steps in Kennebunkport, Maine, to mementos of his leadership during Operation Desert Storm. Another section is dedicated to First Lady Barbara Bush's efforts on behalf of literacy, AIDS prevention, and volunteerism.

SAM HOUSTON
1793 - 1863

The monumental statue of Texas hero Sam Houston (above) at the Huntsville visitors' center can be seen from as far as six miles away. David Adickes created the sixty-seven-foot statue out of thirty tons of steel and concrete. "Old Sparky" (opposite), Texas's infamous electric chair in which 361 inmates were executed from 1924 to 1964, was moved to the Texas Prison Museum in Huntsville in 1989. One doomed convict, J.W. Moore Jr., ordered for his last meal "a small steak, tender, no bone, no fat" plus French fries, butter beans, steak sauce, sliced onion, five large bananas, chocolate ice cream, and one piece of fluffy coconut pie. "Dammit," he wrote, "I want it served hot, and keep it from being mixed up together."

THE TEXAS ELECTRIC CHAIR

"Old Sparky," was used
to execute 361 inmates
from 1924 to 1964. It
was then crated and
stored near the execution
room in the Walls Unit
until it was moved to the
Texas Prison Museum in
April 1989. Executions
were resumed in Texas in
1982 with the lethal
injection method.

Texarkana's post office (above) was constructed on Stateline Avenue—straddling the Texas-Arkansas line. Even the flag of the United States is bisected by the state boundary.

Federal courts for both states convene on their respective sides of the building. Olivia Smith Moore, wife of Texarkana attorney Henry Moore, acquired an impressive shoe col-

lection (opposite), still displayed in the bedroom at Texarkana's famous Draughon-Moore "Ace of Clubs" house. She amassed more than five hundred pairs of shoes, plus

other fine clothing brought to her door by sales representatives from the Neiman-Marcus store in Dallas. Lumberman James Draughon built the home in 1885 in the shape of the ace

of clubs, his lucky card from his days as a Confederate Army captain. According to legend, money to build the house came from a poker game won with the draw of that card.

Country music superstar Clint Black (above) strummed his guitar in front of the courthouse in McKinney, north of Dallas, during the filming of a music video. One of Texas's most impressive courthouses can be found in nearby Denton (opposite), the "North Star of Texas." Others call it "Little D," in contrast to the metropolis down the road. The walls of the 1896 courthouse are native limestone, the columns of Burnett County marble. Architect W. C. Dodson's design is a free combination of Victorian styles. Inside is the Courthouse-on-Square museum, which displays Victorian rooms as well as period guns, pottery, dolls, tools, and blue glass. The museum is also a center for North Texas genealogical research. Dallas's skyline (overleaf) shimmers with the energy that turned "Big D" from a sleepy trading post into one of the nation's most powerful, and architecturally imaginative, business centers seemingly overnight.

After years of shame over the twist of fate that cast it as the site of the 1963 assassination of President John F. Kennedy, Dallas has squarely confronted the memory with a powerful exhibit in the Texas School Book Depository Building (above). Visitors to the Sixth Floor Museum get a full recounting of the events of that November day and an eerily familiar view of Dealey Plaza (left) from the window next to the one from which—according to the official Warren Commission account— lone assassin Lee Harvey Oswald drew a bead on the president and Governor John Connally. The rest of the building houses Dallas County's administration.

A small log cabin (above) was moved from the countryside seven miles outside of town to downtown Dallas, then to its present spot on Historic Square in 1971. Named for settler George Mifflin Dallas of Pennsylvania, Dallas was little more than a post office in the Texas Republic of 1845. Most colonists called the area along the Trinity River "Three Forks," and surely no one dreamed that one day, Dallas would grow into one of the nation's most dynamic supercities. Pioneer Plaza (right) in downtown Dallas is the world's largest bronze monument. Its seventy longhorn steers (forty of which were first unveiled during World Cup soccer festivities in 1994) and three cowboys commemorate the city's western heritage. Robert Summers of Glen Rose, Texas, created the sculptures.

*In Williams Square—the center of the Metroplex's "alternate downtown" in Irving—Robert Glen created the powerful* Mustangs of Las Colinas *sculptures (left) that have become a favorite attraction. The Texas Rangers' intimate, state-of-the-art Ballpark (above) combines with two Six Flags Over Texas theme parks to bring thousands of visitors to Arlington. Billy Bob's Texas in Fort Worth (overleaf)—"The World's Largest Honky Tonk"—opened in 1981 in a building that was once an open-air barn housing prize cattle for the Fort Worth Stock Show. In the 1950s, it became a department store so large that stockboys wore roller skates. For one Hank Williams Jr. concert in the 6,028-seat club, Billy Bob's sold more than sixteen thousand bottles of beer.*

FORT

MAIN
SHOW ROOM

In the same building in McLean that houses the Route 66 Museum is the Devil's Rope Museum (opposite), an exhaustive collection of barbed wire, tools used to stretch it, and sculptures made from it. Indians called barbed wire the "devil's rope" because it restrained their movement; settlers called it "bob wire"; cattlemen cursed it; and range wars were fought where it was strung. Cowboy Mike Dean (above) gets a grip on one of the most bizarre monuments in Texas at the Cadillac Ranch near Amarillo. There, eccentric helium tycoon Stanley Marsh III—with help from a San Francisco design firm called the Ant Farm—buried ten 1949–63 model Cadillacs nose down. The rusting frames soon became a favorite target of graffiti artists. What does it all mean? Guessing is half the fun.

"Trophy buckles" (above)—ornate belt buckles worn by cowboys and often presented as rodeo prizes—are a popular item at Cavender's Boot City western-wear store in Amarillo. Boots (left), of course, which range in price from $39 to more than $1,400, are the biggest sellers. Just about everyone in town wears them everywhere. South of Amarillo is the eight-hundred-foot-deep Palo Duro Canyon (overleaf)—the nation's second-largest canyon—whose copper-colored cliffs are especially spectac- ular at sunset.

PREVIOUS PAGES: Near the state line toward the southeastern corner of New Mexico is Monahans Sandhills State Park, consisting of 3,840 acres of dunes up to seventy feet high. Many are stabilized by vegetation, but bare, active dunes grow and change shape in response to prevailing winds. Branding is a twice-a-year ritual (left) on big cattle spreads like the Ratliff Cross MX Ranch near Odessa. Calves are branded and inoculated against a variety of diseases, and males are castrated. "Jalepeño Sam" Lewis (above) raises and races armadillos like "Tex." The little burrowing mammals, which one wag called "anteaters on the half shell," often become road kill, or "Texas speed bumps," not because they dawdle but because, when cornered by an oncoming car, they tend to hop upward, striking the undercarriage. Midland's wildly popular young Ballet Folk Dancers (overleaf), here performing at Ninfa's Restaurant, learn dance—and self-confidence—at the Hispanic Cultural Center of Midland.

Though "the skies are not cloudy all day" in dry West Texas, roiling clouds mixed with sun are a common sight, as in this scene (opposite) near Saragosa. The Davis Mountains loom in the distance. Rocky crests are closer to the highway in Big Bend National Park (above). The park, which was established along the serpentine curve of the Rio Grande River to protect the fragile Chihuahuan Desert wilderness, covers eleven hundred square miles. The park's vast basins and weathered mountains are full of self-guided trails, but supplies and especially accommodations are relatively scarce. The rugged Chisos Mountains that rise abruptly out of the plains were formed by ancient volcanos. Elsewhere, molten lava squeezed through sedimentary rock to the earth's surface. There is ample evidence throughout the park, too, of violent flash floods. In all, the effect can be awe-inspiring.

*Half the original structures, and many ruins, remain from historic Fort Davis (above) where, from 1854 to 1891, troops based at the post battled Apache and Comanche Indians. They also escorted freight wagons, stagecoaches, and pioneers heading to the new American territories in New Mexico and Arizona on the bleak San Antonio-to-El Paso Trail. The fort was named for Secretary of War— later Confederate president—Jefferson Davis. The Ysleta Mission (opposite) in suburban El Paso was built in 1681 by Franciscan priests and Tigua Indians. The building has been reconstructed but stands on the original foundation and is therefore considered to be the oldest mission in Texas. It is again attended by Tiguas—descendants of the tribe that built it more than three centuries ago.*

*Titles available in the Pictorial Souvenir series*